Acknowledgements

We are grateful to the following
for their permission to reproduce illustrations:

Mary Evans Picture Library—wolf-charmer print
Radio Times Hulton Picture Library—otter-hunting scene
Trustees of the British Museum—Court falconer illustration and beaver print.
The maps of the beaver, otter and wolf are based on maps
which appear in *The Shadow of Extinction* by Jeremy Mallinson, Macmillan 1978.

Cover illustration: Alan R Thomson
Beaver and peregrine illustrations by John Butler,
wolf illustrations by Gwen Fulton
and otter illustrations by Sheila Smith.
Scale drawings by Tim Smith.

We would also like to acknowledge the help received
from the Royal Society for the Protection of Birds.

I want to say three things to you about animals in danger.

You may think that some of these animals are "safe" because you can still see them in zoos and wildlife parks. And it's true that some animals, such as deer, can live fairly natural lives in herds in parks.

But have you ever seen a large family of gorillas in a zoo? No! A gorilla may become bored and unhappy when it's not living in a group - and the babies that are born are often abandoned by their mothers. Gorillas really _need_ to live in large groups in jungles and you can't build a jungle in a zoo.

The first thing I'm saying, then, is that to _truly_ survive, animals must remain in their natural habitat and that these habitats need to be preserved.

My second point is that _people_ have made life difficult for animals. The animals described in this series of books are not necessarily those in the greatest danger, but they've been chosen to show just how many different problems people have made for them. There are now such vast numbers of people on earth that wildlife and wild places are disappearing as we humans take more and more wild land each year.

So the third thing I want to say to you is: we've created these problems, we've put these animals in danger, and now it's up to us to do something about it.

Ray Rourke

© 1982 The Rourke Corporation, Inc.
© W & R Chambers Ltd. 1980

Published by The Rourke Corporation, Inc., P.O. Box 711,
Windermere, Florida 32786. Copyright © 1982 by The Rourke Corporation, Inc. All copyrights reserved.

Library of Congress Cataloging in Publication Data

Animals in danger—Europe
"Produced in association with the Wildlife
Youth Service."
Summary: Brief descriptions of the European
wolf, the otter, the peregrine falcon, and the
European beaver, discussing the precariousness of
their existence in Europe.
1. Endangered species—Europe—Juvenile liter-
ature. 2. Rare animals—Europe—Juvenile liter-
ature. [1. Rare animals—Europe] I. Gould, Gill.
II. Scott, Michael M. III. Butler, John, ill.
IV. Fulton, Gwen, ill. V. Smith, Shelia, ill.
VI. Wildlife Youth Service. VII. Series.
QL84.4.A1D57 1982   333.95'4'094   82-9808
ISBN 0-86592-777-4   AACR2

Children's Reading Institute offers
several cards and activity programs.
For information write to
Children's Reading Institute
Durham, CT 06422

animals
IN DANGER
EUROPE

compiled by Gill Gould

Wildlife adviser Michael M Scott

illustrations by
John Butler, Gwen Fulton and Sheila Smith

THE ROURKE CORPORATION, INC.
Windermere, Florida

THE WOLF

AT RISK

The day before it died, in 1743, the last wolf in Britain is supposed to have attacked — and eaten — two young children in broad daylight. This savage creature was finally killed by a tall, brave hunter named MacQueen, and the local people breathed a sigh of relief.

While it is unlikely that this story is completely true, it is a good example of a 'big bad wolf' story. It shows us how frightened people were of the wolf. They thought of it as a fierce, aggressive animal which would attack a man for no reason at all. Myths about werewolves — people who could change themselves into wolves — were also common. This did not help the wolf's image either, for werewolves were believed to feed on human flesh.

In spite of this, there is no definite evidence that a healthy European wolf has ever killed a human being. Any attacks that have been recorded have probably been made by trapped or injured wolves or by animals suffering from rabies. Wolves are actually afraid of people and will go to great lengths to avoid them.

There are even stranger stories about babies being nursed by wolves — as in the legend of Romulus and Remus, the founders of Rome. It is possible that, a long time ago, wolves were regarded as kindly creatures which were helpful to man.

Wolves like to live in wide open spaces. They organize themselves in packs, which are usually made up of about six to ten animals — larger groups are rare. The pack is a family unit with adults and young. The wolves hunt over a fairly large area, known as their territory, and mark out the boundaries of this area with their scent. Other wolf-packs respect a territory and will rarely enter it.

In order to survive, the pack has to be run very efficiently as a team. The strongest, most aggressive wolf, is the leader. All the other wolves obey their leader's commands. Each wolf has its own particular place in the pack and shows great affection for its fellow members.

Wolves usually hunt at night, although they may have developed this habit in order to avoid man. Before the hunt begins in earnest, the wolves often stand together and howl.

Grey wolf

Red wolf

Man – 1.80 metres tall

o man, this howling of the wolf-pack has always eemed a fearful sound. In fact, it appears to be the olf's way of communicating with others in the ack, and perhaps of warning other wolf-packs to tay away.

he grey wolf of Europe and North America is the nost common type of wolf. The smaller red wolf, vhich is found only in Texas and Louisiana, is now xtremely rare. Wolves belong to the same family of nimals as coyotes — which are small wolves — ackals, foxes and domestic dogs. Although often alled the Tasmanian wolf, the striped thylacine — ne of those animals which has almost certainly ecome extinct this century — belonged to a ifferent family altogether. It was one of the ouched mammals, like the kangaroos and koalas.

FACT BOX

Wolf

Canis lupus

Family Canidae, the dog family.
Range North America, Russia and Central Asia. Now extinct over most of western Europe, although still found in eastern European countries.
Habitat Wooded plains and mountains, also more open country.
Food Mostly large mammals — reindeer, horses, cattle and sheep.
Young 5–6 cubs born in spring, 7 weeks after mating.

Alsatian

Coyote

Thylacine

Once found over most of Europe, North America and parts of Asia, the wolf is now becoming scarce in many places. It is very rare in western Europe and is extinct in eleven European countries.

In Britain wolves had always been hunted because of the damage they did to flocks of sheep and many laws were passed to control what was known as the 'wolf plague'. People really believed that they could not live side by side with the wolf — so it had to be destroyed.

As late as 1970 sums of money, or bounties, were paid for dead wolves in Finland, although there were very few wolves left there. In some countries poisoned bait is still put down for wolves. So we see that the old idea of man and the wolf being unable to share the same land still exists.

Like the pied piper of Hamelin, who could charm rats out of the town with his music, people believed in the existence of 'wolf-charmers' up to the end of the nineteenth century.

Conservation groups are now trying to change this. The World Wildlife Fund has organized a campaign throughout Europe to try to help people, and governments, to understand the wolf better. In this way they hope that complete protection may be given to the species.

In Italy, where there are about a hundred wolves, the World Wildlife Fund's 'Operation St Francis' is trying to save them. Some of the wolves have been fitted with collars with radio transmitters attached, so that their movements can be studied. In following the wolves, the research team learn more about their habits, their behaviour and the size of the area they travel over. One of the researchers worked out the number of wolves in the area by copying the wolf's howl. The wolves howled back their response and a record was kept of each separate howl. Thanks to the information they have gathered, the wolf has now been given complete protection in Italy.

The future of the wolf in Europe depends on our attitude towards it. It can still be saved, but only if we really want to save it. People's feelings towards the wolf are beginning to change, but will they change in time? How do you think you would feel if there were wolves living near you?

THE OTTER

Few people have seen more of an otter than the streak of bubbles that follows behind it as it swims at speed underwater. Otters are shy, cautious animals and usually come out only at night, especially in areas where they are hunted or likely to be disturbed.

They live in lakes, rivers, streams — wherever the water is clean and they are left in peace. They are also often found along rocky western coasts, for what is known as the 'sea otter' of Europe is not in fact a different animal at all.

They shelter by day in holes in the river bank, in old drains, or amongst the roots of riverside trees. The breeding den or 'holt' is in a similar place and is usually lined with reeds and grass. Here the cubs are born and spend their first two months.

Otters can be very playful, making slides down banks of mud or snow, and stopping to investigate any strange objects they find. Cubs especially will twist and turn with great speed in the water as they play 'tag', and will sometimes dive to the bottom of the river for pebbles which they play with like toys.

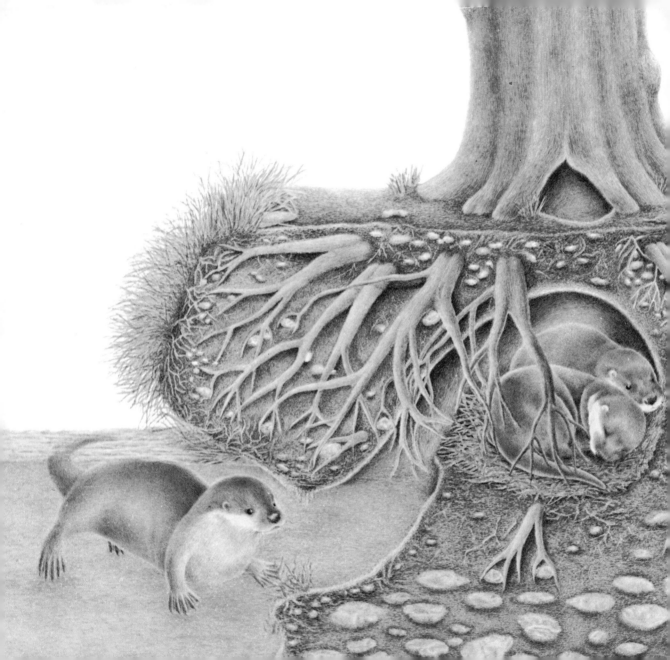

The otter is beautifully designed as an underwater hunter. Shaped like a torpedo, it can reach speeds of 10 kilometres an hour underwater. It swims by waving its body, like a snake moving on land. The webbed feet help when it needs a burst of speed, and the flattened tail is used as a rudder for steering.

When the otter dives its nostrils close, but it can hold its breath underwater for up to four minutes and travel up to 400 metres. On land its senses of smell and hearing are very good. But when it dives with its ears and nostrils closed, it must rely on its eyesight. Its whiskers may also help it to sense the movement of its prey, and to find its way in cloudy water.

Approaching with speed, an otter catches fish from underneath, often using its front paws. There is no doubt that it does kill trout and salmon from time to time. This upsets fishermen and gamekeepers, some of whom still set traps for the otter. However, scientists have shown that its main food is fish such as perch and pike, which are no use to fishermen. Where eels are common, the otter will kill large numbers of these. As eels feed on salmon and trout eggs, the otter may well be helping the fishermen by killing eels.

Man – 1.80 metres tall

FACT BOX

Otter
Lutra lutra

Family Mustelidae, the weasel family.
Range Scattered over Europe, most of Asia and Northern Africa.
Habitat Lakes, marshes, rivers and streams. Also seacoast and islands.
Food Fish, crabs, frogs, snails and small birds and mammals.
Young Usually 2–3 cubs, born at any time of the year. The family usually stays together for about a year. The cubs first enter the water at 10 weeks.

Otters can certainly do a lot of damage at fish hatcheries, but surely it is simply up to us to keep the otter out. We can hardly blame the otter for being tempted by a lot of young fish just waiting to be eaten!

The otter holt, often made amongst the roots of trees, usually has two entrances, one of which opens out underwater so that the mother can approach the nest without being seen.

Nineteenth century otter-hunt using long spears.
Otter-hunting is now controlled in England and Wales,
but not in Scotland.

HOW POLLUTION AFFECTS THE OTTER

In some countries, otters are still hunted for what is called 'sport'. They are literally 'hounded' by twenty to forty terriers, sometimes for up to five hours, until they are either forced onto land or into shallow water to be killed. The otter skin is not worth very much, so sometimes the otter is allowed to escape. However, many otters may then die of sheer fright, and the disturbance to otters and all other river life by the hunt can be very serious.

All the same, the huntsmen do not kill very many otters. The main threat is far more serious. The otter is steadily losing more and more of the places where it can live as towns spread farther and farther along the river banks and as streams are controlled and dammed. Power boats and cruisers on the rivers and picnickers on the banks scare it away from still more rivers. Above all, the pollution, or poisoning, of rivers by sewage, waste from factories and from chemicals now makes it impossible for the otter to live in many places. Only where it is farthest from man is the otter still safe — but for how much longer?

In Britain and elsewhere, there are plans to set aside 'otter havens', stretches of river which will be kept as clean, natural and undisturbed as possible, so that the otter can live there safely. Conservation groups are working together to find out more about the otter's life so that it can be better protected. At last attempts are being made to clean up the rivers.

Pollution, after all, affects not just the otter but all life in the river. That includes the trout and salmon which the hunters once said they were protecting by killing the otter. Now these hunters and others will have to try instead to protect trout, salmon *and* otter, by protecting the river itself.

PEREGRINE FALCON

AT RISK

To the ancient Egyptians the falcon was a holy bird. One of their sky-gods, Horus — whose name means 'he who is on high' — is often shown in their paintings and sculptures in the shape of a peregrine falcon.

It is easy to see why the Egyptians thought so highly of the peregrine. Although fairly small, about the size of a crow, its fierce, alert appearance makes up for its lack of size. Like all birds of prey, it has powerful talons with which to catch its food and a razor-sharp beak to tear the flesh up. The male bird is known as the tiercel. The female, simply called the falcon, is much bigger than the male and may weigh twice as much as he does.

Peregrines like to wander from place to place — to peregrinate means to travel about — and so they can be seen in almost any type of countryside. Most of the time they live alone, but during the breeding season each bird chooses a mate and they stay together until the end of the season.

The falcon lays her eggs in a hollow on a high cliff or mountain ledge or perhaps in the old nest of a raven or some other bird. The chicks hatch out in late spring.

At first the chicks are quite helpless, but by the time they are a few weeks old they can tear up the food their parents bring them. Once the young birds can fly, their parents take them out every day and teach them to hunt and kill for themselves.

Peregrines catch their prey in flight. They have very sharp eyesight and can spot a victim from some distance away. They attack swiftly, diving down and striking their prey to the ground. This action is known as the peregrine's 'stoop'. When a skilful peregrine 'stoops', it is one of the fastest of all birds and can reach the amazing speed of 300 kilometres per hour.

FACT BOX

Peregrine falcon

Falco peregrinus

Family Falconidae, the falcon family.
Range Scattered over most of Europe, North America, Asia and Australia.
Habitat Usually wild, open country — mountains, moors, near sea cliffs.
Food Birds of all sizes, including pigeons, ducks and small gamebirds. Also rabbits and other small mammals.
Eggs 3 or 4 eggs are laid in April. The eggs hatch out after about 4 weeks.

Man – 1.80 metres tall

In the early 1960s, it was discovered that many peregrines were dying mysteriously. The cause was finally traced to chemicals — such as DDT and dieldrin — which were used on grain crops to kill insects. Pigeons and other birds fed on the treated grain and the peregrine then ate these birds. The poison built up inside the peregrine's body as it ate more and more birds. Hundreds of peregrines died as a result.

In Britain, the use of the most harmful chemicals is now controlled. This means that the danger to the peregrine is not so great and their numbers are beginning to build up again, but in most parts of Europe chemicals are still used freely and the peregrine is still in danger.

Many female peregrines laid eggs with very thin shells as a result of eating pigeons which had fed on grain treated with chemicals. The eggs broke under the weight of the parent bird before the chicks were able to hatch out.

All sorts of other dangers face the peregrine — egg collectors, gamekeepers guarding their grouse, and falconers looking for peregrine chicks to train.

Falconry is the sport in which falcons and other birds of prey are used to hunt game. It first became popular in eastern countries centuries ago, even before man learned to write. Merchants and travellers returning from the East brought the sport to Europe. The peregrine was one of the most popular falcons and was the bird which was used by kings.

In those days there were fairly large numbers of peregrines, so no one worried too much about chicks being taken from their nests. Today things are very different, for the peregrine is now rare throughout the whole of its range.

In Britain the Bird Protection Act allows only falconers with proper permits to remove chicks from eyries. In recent years very few permits have been given. Many other countries have similar laws.

Sixteenth century Persian court falconer with a falcon on his wrist.

Unfortunately, there are still people who are ready to break these laws and in some places raids by falconers have greatly reduced the numbers of wild peregrines. In one year about a fifth of the nests, or eyries, in the United Kingdom were robbed by egg thieves and falconers.

In the United States, birds have been bred in captivity and then returned to areas where peregrines had been wiped out by DDT. Young birds were put into the nests of wild peregrines whose own eggs had not hatched. Others were raised in captivity and then carefully trained back to the wild.

The peregrine is now in danger in most European countries. In Britain it appears to be recovering, thanks to the protection there. In other countries peregrines could certainly be helped by the same sort of protection. We should also learn from the story of the peregrine that the uncontrolled use of chemicals in farming may be harmful not only to all kinds of wildlife, but perhaps also to man.

Egyptian vulture

Bonelli's eagle

Snowy owl

Peregrine falcon

All of these birds of prey are now in danger

EUROPEAN BEAVER

RECOVERING THROUGH PROTECTION

Apart from man, no other animal is able to change the landscape as much as the beaver. Working in groups they fell trees, from which they build dams to control the flow of their rivers, and dig canals to carry logs back to their homes. Sometimes their dams can be huge, more than 600 metres wide.

Beavers usually sleep during the day and come out around sunset. They like to live in wooded places near streams, rivers and lakes.

Although they look rather clumsy when they are walking on land, they are good swimmers and can stay underwater for fifteen minutes if necessary.

Man – 1.80 metres tall

FACT BOX

European beaver
Castor fiber

Family Castoridae, the beaver family, which includes the American beaver.
Range Scattered mostly over northern and eastern Europe.
Habitat Near rivers, lakes and streams in woods and forests.
Food Mostly the bark of trees, also water-plants, leaves, twigs and seeds.
Young 2–5 young are born in the spring, 9–12 weeks after mating.

Beavers live together in family groups. The young stay with their parents until they are two years old, then the adult beavers chase them away so that they may start their own colonies.

The beaver's home is either a burrow in the river bank or a 'lodge' — which you can see in the illustration opposite — built out of twigs, branches and mud. Both types have underwater entrances. The lodge usually has one circular 'room' which is where the beavers sleep. This is also where the young spend the first few weeks of their lives. In the top part of the lodge the mud and twigs are less densely packed so that some air is allowed through.

Beavers build dams to control the water level round their homes. The dam is made from felled trees, which the beaver gnaws through with the front teeth which keep growing throughout its life.

Drawing of a beaver from
a seventeenth century book

The beaver was once common throughout Europe, parts of Asia and North America. It was of great importance to the early hunting tribes, who ate beaver meat and used the fur to make clothing.

Different parts of the beaver were made into medicines. Most valuable of all was castoreum, a scented substance the beaver produces from special glands in its body and uses to mark the borders of its territory. This substance was believed to cure almost any kind of sickness — from headaches to madness. Castoreum is still used in perfumes and cosmetics.

The fashion for beaverskin hats, a fashion which lasted for several centuries, did not help the beaver. Beaverskin was preferred to any other kind of fur because it was water-repellent and kept the wearer's head dry. After the beaver had become extinct in Britain, around the twelfth century, the fur for the hats was bought from other countries in Europe.

Place names such as Beverley, in England, probably mean 'stream inhabited by beavers', and are often all that remain to show that beavers once lived there.

The beaver became extinct in Switzerland during the eighteenth century and was wiped out in Sweden and Finland about a hundred years later. Early this century the beaver was in great danger of becoming extinct throughout Europe.

In the past thirty years or so people have tried to return beavers to their old homes. This project has been successful, and the beaver has been re-introduced to countries such as Sweden, Germany, Switzerland and the areas of the USSR where it had become extinct. Fifty years ago there were only a few hundred beavers left in Europe — now there are several thousand. The beaver is protected wherever it is found.

Beavers have often been accused of being destructive animals which destroy the landscape and eat the bark of valuable trees. Slowly we are beginning to realize that they can help us. Their dams keep rivers flowing evenly and prevent floods, and most of the trees they feed on — birch, willow and elder — are of little use to man.

Perhaps one day beavers will be brought back to all the areas in which they used to live in Europe. Certainly there are many people at present who would like to see the beaver brought back to Britain.

Red squirrel

Some other rodents. A rodent is an animal which gnaws its food.

Beaver

Coypu

Guinea pig

Hamster

APPROXIMATE RANGE OF THE ANIMALS

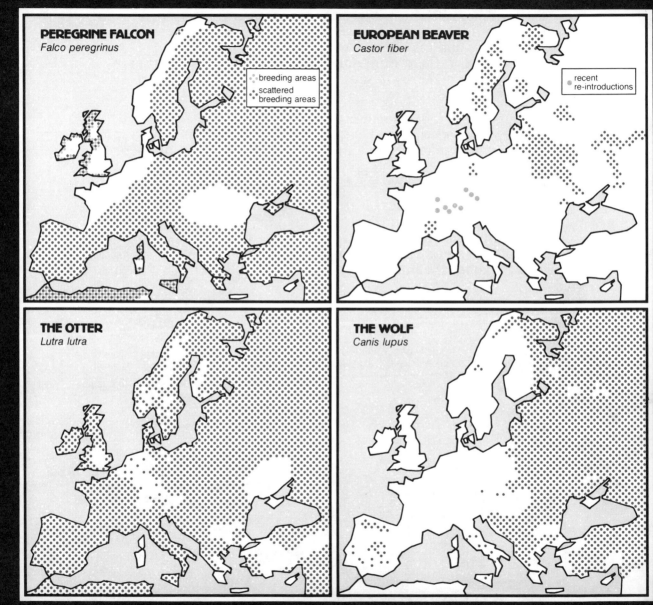

PEREGRINE FALCON
Falco peregrinus

breeding areas
scattered breeding areas

EUROPEAN BEAVER
Castor fiber

recent re-introductions

THE OTTER
Lutra lutra

THE WOLF
Canis lupus